I love Jayson b

I love myself because...

I love myself because...

_____
_____
_____
_____
_____
_____
_____
_____
_____
_____
_____
_____
_____
_____
_____
_____
_____
_____
_____
_____
_____

I love myself because...

_____

_____

_____

_____

_____

_____

_____

_____

_____

_____

_____

_____

_____

_____

_____

_____

_____

_____

_____

_____

_____

_____

Things that make me happy

Things that make me happy

Things that make me happy

Things that make me happy

All the good things in my life

_____

_____

_____

_____

_____

_____

_____

_____

_____

_____

_____

_____

_____

_____

_____

_____

_____

_____

_____

_____

All the good things in my life

All the good things in my life

All the good things in my life

All the good things in my life

Notes to my future self

Notes to my future self

Notes to my future self

_____
_____
_____
_____
_____
_____
_____
_____
_____
_____
_____
_____
_____
_____
_____
_____
_____
_____
_____
_____
_____

Whinging area

I hereby promise to write all my whingy thoughts here then smile and let them go
because they're not worth it

_____

_____

_____

_____

_____

_____

_____

_____

_____

_____

_____

_____

_____

_____

_____

_____

_____

_____

_____

_____

Whinging area

I hereby promise to write all my whingy thoughts here then smile and let them go
because they're not worth it

Whinging area

I hereby promise to write all my whingy thoughts here then smile and let them go
because they're not worth it

_____

_____

_____

_____

_____

_____

_____

_____

_____

_____

_____

_____

_____

_____

_____

_____

_____

_____

_____

_____

_____

Whinging area

**I hereby promise to write all my whingy thoughts here then smile and let them go
because they're not worth it**

Whinging area

I hereby promise to write all my whingy thoughts here then smile and let them go
because they're not worth it

Whinging area

**I hereby promise to write all my whingy thoughts here then smile and let them go
because they're not worth it**

_____

_____

_____

_____

_____

_____

_____

_____

_____

_____

_____

_____

_____

_____

_____

_____

_____

_____

_____

Whinging area

I hereby promise to write all my whingy thoughts here then smile and let them go
because they're not worth it

Prioritising this today will give me time...

Boring Priority	Fun Activity

Prioritising this today will give me time to...

Boring Priority	Fun Activity

Prioritising this today will give me time to...

Boring Priority	Fun Activity

Prioritising this today will give me time to...

Boring Priority	Fun Activity

Decisions, decisions, decisions

Pros | Cons

Decisions, decisions, decisions

Pros

Cons

Decisions, decisions, decisions

Pros   **Cons**

Decisions, decisions, decisions

Pros	Cons

Decisions, decisions, decisions

Pros	Cons

Notes & Doodles

Notes & Doodles

Notes & Doodles

Notes & Doodles

Notes & Doodles

Notes & Doodles

Notes & Doodles

Notes & Doodles

Notes & Doodles

Notes & Doodles

Notes & Doodles

Notes & Doodles

Notes & Doodles

Notes & Doodles

Notes & Doodles

Notes & Doodles

Notes & Doodles

Notes & Doodles

Notes & Doodles

Notes & Doodles

Notes & Doodles

Notes & Doodles

Notes & Doodles

Notes & Doodles

Notes & Doodles

Notes & Doodles

Notes & Doodles

Notes & Doodles

Notes & Doodles

Notes & Doodles

Notes & Doodles

Notes & Doodles

Notes & Doodles

Notes & Doodles

Notes & Doodles

Notes & Doodles

Notes & Doodles

Notes & Doodles

Printed in Great Britain
by Amazon

57599564R00041